Passing the PRINCE2 Examinations

The APM Group,
based on the original book
by Ken Bradley

London: TSO

Published by TSO (The Stationery Office) and available from:

Online
www.tso.co.uk/bookshop

Mail, Telephone, Fax & E-mail
TSO
PO Box 29, Norwich, NR3 1GN
Telephone orders/General enquiries: 0870 600 5522
Fax orders: 0870 600 5533
E-mail: book.orders@tso.co.uk
Textphone 0870 240 3701

TSO Shops
123 Kingsway, London, WC2B 6PQ
020 7242 6393 Fax 020 7242 6394
68-69 Bull Street, Birmingham B4 6AD
0121 236 9696 Fax 0121 236 9699
9-21 Princess Street, Manchester M60 8AS
0161 834 7201 Fax 0161 833 0634
16 Arthur Street, Belfast BT1 4GD
028 9023 8451 Fax 028 9023 5401
18-19 High Street, Cardiff CF10 1PT
029 2039 5548 Fax 029 2038 4347
71 Lothian Road, Edinburgh EH3 9AZ
0870 606 5566 Fax 0870 606 5588

TSO Accredited Agents
(see Yellow Pages)

and through good booksellers

The information contained in this publication is believed to be correct at the
time of manufacture. Whilst care has been taken to ensure that the information
is accurate, the publisher can accept no responsibility for any errors or
omissions or for changes to the details given.

PRINCE® is a Registered Trade Mark of the Office of Government Commerce
and Registered in U.S. Patent and Trademark Office

The PRINCE2 logo ™ is a Trade Mark of the Office of Government Commerce

A CIP catalogue record for this book is available from the British Library
A Library of Congress CIP catalogue record has been applied for

First published 2004

ISBN 0 11 330964 3

Printed in the United Kingdom by The Stationery Office
ID170396 06/04 C30 19585 977449

Contents

Foreword

This book is aimed at easing the path for all those intending to take the APM Group PRINCE2 foundation and practitioner examinations. Those taking the APM Group Practitioner Re-Registration Examination will find that the advice provided is equally relevant and useful. *Passing the PRINCE2 Examinations* has been updated to reflect changes to the PRINCE2 reference manual released early in 2002.

Thanks go to the APM Group and the PRINCE2 Examination Board for allowing the use of PRINCE2 examination material, and Richard Pharro for his support and encouragement in getting this publication to print.

I hope you will find this book of real use in preparing for, and passing, your examinations. The royalties from this book go to the APM Group annual PRINCE2 award scheme – full details of which can be obtained from the APM Group.

This is a complementary, not a 'core', publication on PRINCE2 and, therefore, is not endorsed by the PRINCE2 Examination Board.

Based on the original book by Ken Bradley

December 2003

The Foundation and Practitioner Joint Syllabus (2002)

The ticks in the right-hand columns in the syllabus below show what topics are included in the two examinations. This syllabus is correct at the time of going to press. This can be checked by accessing the PRINCE2.ORG website, which always contains the latest version of the syllabus.

Contents

Introduction

Syllabus

Overview and principles

Organisation

Business Case

Controls

Change Control

The Management of Risk

Quality in a project environment

Plans

Configuration management

Processes

Product-based planning

Quality review

Introduction

This syllabus is designed to provide a basis for accreditation of project management professionals. The syllabus is based on the CCTA publication *Managing Successful Projects* (1989) and is intended to provide a basis for setting examinations at Foundation and Practitioner levels and to guide assessment at Professional level. The following table describes the competence required at each level.

Foundation	Candidates must be able to describe the purpose of all roles, processes, deliverables.
	Candidates must be able to identify which deliverables are input and output from which processes.
	Candidates must be able to identify the relationships between processes, deliverables, roles and the management dimensions of a project.
Practitioner	Candidates must exhibit all competence required for the Foundation qualification.
	For a given project scenario candidates must be able to produce detailed explanations of all processes, components and techniques, and worked examples of all management products.
	Candidates must be able to show they understand the relationships between PRINCE2 processes, components, techniques, project management products, roles and the management dimensions of a project, and can apply this understanding in practice in project management.
	Candidates must be able to demonstrate that they understand the reasons behind the various elements of PRINCE2, and that they understand the principles underpinning these elements.
	Candidates must be able to demonstrate their ability to tune PRINCE2 to different project circumstances.
	Candidates must be able to demonstrate an understanding of projects in context, with business operations and programmes.

The syllabus will also inform the design, development and use of training materials and courses aimed at raising an individual's understanding of and competence in the project management approach as described in *Managing Successful Projects*.

The syllabus has been designed with ease of reference, extensibility and ease of maintenance in mind. The structure of the syllabus is depicted in Figure 1.

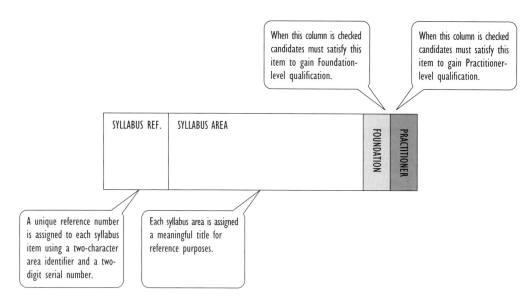

Figure 1 Syllabus Structure

Syllabus

Syllabus Reference		Syllabus Area	Foundation	Practitioner
Overview and principles				
OV	01	Candidates should be able to identify the typical characteristics of a project.	✓	✓
OV	02	Candidates should be able to identify the benefits of a structured approach to project management.	✓	✓
OV	03	Each candidate should be able to identify the relationship between the project environment and the daily business of an organisation.	✓	✓
OV	04	Candidates should be able to identify the differences between the project life cycle and the product lifespan.	✓	✓
OV	05	Candidates should be able to identify what part of a product lifespan is covered by PRINCE2.	✓	✓
OV	06	Candidates should be able to identify the main elements of PRINCE2, including all processes, components and techniques.	✓	✓
OV	07	Candidates should understand PRINCE2 terminology, including customer, supplier, user, product, Business Case, exception and stage.	✓	✓
OV	08	Candidates should be able to describe the justification for, and benefits arising from using *Managing Successful Projects* in a given scenario.		✓
Organisation				
OR	01	Candidates should be able to distinguish between the management and the direction of a project.	✓	✓
OR	02	Candidates can identify the four layers in the PRINCE2 project organisation.	✓	✓

Syllabus Reference		Syllabus Area	Foundation	Practitioner
OR	03	Candidates can recognise the Business, User and Supplier interests of participating parties in a project.	✓	✓
OR	04	Candidates should be able to identify the roles of a typical PRINCE2 project organisation structure as described in *Managing Successful Projects*.	✓	✓
OR	05	Candidates should be able to describe the typical project organisation structure as described in *Managing Successful Projects*.		✓
OR	06	Candidates should understand in detail the purpose and responsibilities of the Project Manager, Project Assurance, Team Manager and Project Support.	✓	✓
OR	07	Candidates should understand the Project Board roles in detail.		✓
OR	08	Candidates should be able to produce the design of an appropriate organisation for a given scenario, applying all roles as identified in *Managing Successful Projects*, with explanations of the responsibilities of each role and of the reporting and information flow relationships between roles for that particular scenario.		✓
OR	09	Candidates should be able to describe in detail the typical and potential functions of the Project Support and Team Manager roles.	✓	✓
OR	10	Candidates should be able to produce Role Descriptions for the Project Board, Project Manager, Team Manager, Project Assurance and Project Support for a given project scenario.		✓
OR	11	Candidates should be able to identify the acceptable consolidations or sharing of roles as described in *Managing Successful Projects*.		✓
OR	12	Candidates should be able to apply acceptable role consolidations/sharing and their resultant organisation structure to a given scenario.		✓

Business Case

			Foundation	Practitioner
BN	01	Candidates should be able to identify the fundamental importance of the benefits focus of PRINCE2 in project management.	✓	✓
BN	02	Candidates should be able to describe the fundamental importance of the benefits focus of PRINCE2 in project management.		✓
BN	03	Candidates should understand the various sections of the Business Case, where in the project processes these are created, updated and monitored, and the purpose of each activity with relation to Benefits Management.		✓
BN	04	Candidates should be able to list the factors that would be considered in the development of the Business Case.		✓
BN	05	Candidates should be able to create an outline Business Case from information provided in a scenario.		✓
BN	06	Candidates should be able to perform a simple Investment Appraisal based on information provided in a scenario.		✓

Syllabus Reference		Syllabus Area	Foundation	Practitioner

Controls

CO	01	Candidates should be able to identify the objectives of control in a project context.	✓	✓
CO	02	Candidates should be able to identify the products involved in the controlled start of a project and explain the PID.	✓	✓
CO	03	Candidates should be able to identify the various ingredients of controlled progress in a project and understand the concepts of the following: tolerance, Product Descriptions, Work Packages, Checkpoint and Highlight Reports and Project Issues.	✓	✓
CO	04	Candidates should understand the reasons for breaking a project into stages and understand the difference between management and technical stages.	✓	✓
CO	05	Candidates should be able to identify the products involved in bringing a project to a controlled close.	✓	✓
CO	06	Candidates should be able to demonstrate the links between the elements of the Controls component and the processes in which they are used.		✓
CO	07	Candidates should be able to describe in detail each control product, its purpose, who is involved and when it is created and updated.		✓
CO	08	Candidates should be able to apply the various PRINCE2 controls for the Project Board or the Project Manager to a given scenario.		✓

Change Control

CC	01	Candidates should understand the purpose of Change Control.	✓	✓
CC	02	Candidates should be able to identify the documents and general administration of Project Issues.	✓	✓
CC	03	Candidates should understand the link between Change Control and Configuration Management.	✓	✓
CC	04	Candidates should understand the PRINCE2 Approach to Change Control.	✓	✓
CC	05	Candidates should be able to identify the typical Change Control activities of the Project Manager and Project Support in each project process.	✓	✓
CC	06	Candidates should be able to describe the typical Change Control activities of the Project Manager and Project Support in each project process.		✓
CC	07	Candidates should be able to apply the typical Change Control activities for all relevant roles for each project process to a given scenario.		✓
CC	08	Candidates should be able to devise a method for Change Control based on the PRINCE2 approach and the needs of a given scenario.		✓
CC	09	Candidates should be able to discuss the factors determining escalation of Project Issues to the Project Board, identify the processes involved and create the products required, based on a given scenario.		✓

Syllabus Reference		Syllabus Area	Foundation	Practitioner

The Management of Risk

RK	01	Candidates should be able to identify the importance of Management of Risk for a project and when it should be performed as described in *Managing Successful Projects*.	✓	✓
RK	02	Candidates should understand the purpose and main elements of the Management of Risk as described in *Managing Successful Projects*.	✓	✓
RK	03	Candidates should be able to describe the purpose and main elements of the Management of Risk as described in *Managing Successful Projects*.		✓
RK	04	Candidates should be able to demonstrate the ability to apply the PRINCE2 approach to the Management of Risk to a given scenario.		✓
RK	05	Candidates should be able to select appropriate risks from the Risk Category Appendix for a given scenario.		✓
RK	06	Candidates should understand the relationship between risk, Business Case, plans and Project Issues.		✓
RK	07	Candidates should be able to describe the purpose of the Risk Log, when it is created and updated.	✓	✓
RK	08	Candidates should be able to create a Risk Log and make entries in it from a given scenario.		✓
RK	09	Candidates should be able to demonstrate the interfaces between the Management of Risk component, the processes and all other relevant areas of *Managing Successful Projects*.		✓

Quality in a project environment

QU	01	Candidates should be able to describe the purpose and main elements of Quality Management as described in *Managing Successful Projects*.		✓
QU	02	Candidates should be able to describe the quality path through a project as illustrated in *Managing Successful Projects*.		✓
QU	03	Candidates should understand the importance of the customer's quality expectations.	✓	✓
QU	04	Candidates should be able to demonstrate understanding of the work of an organisation's quality assurance and the link to the Project Assurance role in a PRINCE2 project.		✓
QU	05	Candidates should be able to describe the typical Quality Management responsibilities and activities of the Project Board, Project Manager, Team Manager and Project Assurance role for each project process as described in *Managing Successful Projects*.		✓

Syllabus Reference		Syllabus Area	Foundation	Practitioner
QU	06	Candidates should understand the part played by a possible quality management system from the user or supplier in contributing to a project's Project Quality Plan.	✓	✓
QU	07	Candidates should be able to propose measures to specify, monitor and control the quality of products in a PRINCE2 project.		✓
QU	08	Candidates should be able to create any of the quality products described in *Managing Successful Projects* based on a given scenario.		✓
QU	09	Candidates must understand the impact of any quality product on other products.		✓

Plans

			Foundation	Practitioner
PL	01	Candidates should be able to demonstrate understanding of what a plan is, its structure and the levels of plan as described in *Managing Successful Projects*.	✓	✓
PL	02	Candidates should be able to describe in outline the purpose of the Project Plan, Stage Plan, Team Plan and Exception Plan and indicate when these plans are created.		✓
PL	03	Candidates should be able to describe the necessity and advantages of making a plan.		✓
PL	04	Candidates should be able to describe the interrelationship between the Project Plan, Stage Plans, Team Plans and an Exception Plan.		✓
PL	05	Candidates should be able to examine and discuss a plan from a given scenario.		✓

Configuration management

			Foundation	Practitioner
CM	01	Candidates should understand the basic configuration management procedures as described in *Managing Successful Projects*.	✓	✓
CM	02	Candidates should be able to describe the purpose of project-level configuration management as described in *Managing Successful Projects*.		✓
CM	03	Candidates should be able to apply the process of configuration management as described in *Managing Successful Projects* to a given scenario.		✓
CM	04	Candidates should be able to demonstrate understanding of the interfaces between configuration management and the processes.	✓	✓
CM	05	Candidates should be able to discuss in detail the process of establishing and operating configuration management to a given scenario.		✓
CM	06	Candidates should understand the Configuration Librarian role in detail.	✓	✓
CM	07	Candidates should understand the relationship between configuration management and change control.	✓	✓
CM	08	Candidates should be able to explain the relationship required between project configuration management method and the customer's configuration management method for operational products.	✓	✓

Syllabus Reference		Syllabus Area	Foundation	Practitioner
CM	09	Candidates should be capable of creating a configuration record based on information in a given scenario.		✓
CM	10	Candidates should understand version control and the reasons for it.	✓	✓
CM	11	Candidates should be capable of proposing coding schemes for the purposes of identification of configuration records and versions.		✓
CM	12	Candidates should understand the PRINCE2 filing structure and identify where the various management products should be filed.	✓	✓
CM	13	Candidates should be capable of discussing the elements to be considered when designing the configuration management method for a project in a given scenario.		✓

Processes

			Foundation	Practitioner
PR	01	The candidate should know the eight PRINCE2 processes and their normal sequence.	✓	✓
PR	02	The candidate should understand the objectives, inputs and outputs for each of the eight processes.	✓	✓
PR	03	Candidates should understand the sub-processes of 'Controlling a Stage' and 'Managing Product Delivery' as described in *Managing Successful Projects*.	✓	✓
PR	04	Candidates should be able to describe the sub-processes and main steps involved in the carrying out of each of the processes as described in *Managing Successful Projects*.		✓
PR	05	Candidates should be able to demonstrate the application of the processes as described in *Managing Successful Projects*, their interfaces and inter-dependencies, for a given project scenario.		✓
PR	06	Candidates should be able to describe in detail the objective, nature and relevant responsibilities of each project role in each of the major processes.		✓
PR	07	Candidates should be able to discuss in detail the passage of the various management products through the processes.		✓

Product-based planning

			Foundation	Practitioner
PP	01	The candidate should know the steps involved in product-based planning.	✓	✓
PP	02	The candidate should understand the benefits of product-based planning.	✓	✓
PP	03	Candidates should know where in the processes product-based planning is used as described in *Managing Successful Projects*.	✓	✓
PP	04	Candidates should be able to relate the product-based planning technique to the sub-processes of the Planning process.		✓
PP	05	Candidates should be able to draw a Product Breakdown Structure and Product Flow Diagram for a given scenario.		✓

Syllabus Reference		Syllabus Area	Foundation	Practitioner
PP	06	Candidates should be able to demonstrate understanding of the hierarchical rules involved in drawing up a correct Product Breakdown Structure.		✓
PP	07	Candidates should be able to demonstrate understanding of the use/non-use of intermediate Product Breakdown Structure products in the Product Flow Diagram.		✓
PP	08	Candidates should be able to write a Product Description for a product identified in a scenario.	✓	✓
PP	09	Candidates should be able to demonstrate understanding of the rules involved in indicating and using external products.		✓

Quality review

			Foundation	Practitioner
QR	01	The candidate should know the three steps of a quality review.	✓	✓
QR	02	The candidate should know the roles used in a quality review.	✓	✓
QR	03	Candidates should know the various products used in a quality review.	✓	✓
QR	04	Candidates should know the purpose and benefits of a quality review and the type of products for which PRINCE2 recommends its use.	✓	✓
QR	05	Candidates should know where quality reviews are planned and the various roles of the project management team involved in their planning.	✓	✓
QR	06	Candidates should be able to describe in detail the quality review procedure.		✓
QR	07	Candidates should be able to discuss in detail the links between a quality review, the processes and project management team roles.		✓

The Foundation Examination

What is the examination?

The Foundation Examination is a one-hour, closed-book examination. It is designed to test the candidate's knowledge of the PRINCE2 method by choosing the correct answer from a selection of possible answers. There are 75 questions in all and candidates must score 38 correct answers or more to pass. There is no consolidation or carry-forward of time or scores to the Practitioner Examination – the Foundation Examination stands alone. Candidates intending to take the PRINCE2 Practitioner Examination (or any other PRINCE-related examination) must first pass the Foundation Examination.

The track record

Statistics released by the APM Group to PRINCE2 Accredited Training Organisations (ATOs) show that around 95% of all candidates pass the Foundation Examination, indicating that the level of understanding of the PRINCE2 terminology and overview of the method is high.

The Practitioner Examination requires candidates to demonstrate that they are able to apply the method to a project situation. Only around 65% of candidates taking the Registered Practitioner Examination reach the required standard, indicating that the examination is quite a tough test of their ability to take a project scenario and answer questions on how to apply the PRINCE2 method. The third part of this publication provides advice and guidance on the Practitioner Examination.

There is an interesting correlation between marks scored in the Foundation Examination and success in the Practitioner Examination – essentially the more marks scored in the Foundation Examination, the higher the success rate at practitioner level. Candidates who pass the Foundation Examination with 38–40 marks are, statistically, much less likely to pass the Practitioner Examination; those with Foundation Examination scores in excess of 70 marks almost always pass the Practitioner Examination.

The examination questions

On the following pages are examples of the questions and multiple-choice answers that make up the Foundation Examination. Do not approach the questions 'cold'; you must have done quite a bit of preparation before attempting any, otherwise you will get demoralised!

There are over 450 questions in the APM Group database from which the actual examination questions are taken. Some of the questions are very straightforward and will give you little trouble; others drill down into the method and are there to really test your knowledge. You will find that some of the possible answers posed can be eliminated even with a basic knowledge of the method.

Preparing for the examination

Success in the Foundation Examination requires a good understanding of PRINCE2 terminology, an overview of the method and the flows of information within it. The official PRINCE2 manual (*Managing Successful Projects with PRINCE2* ISBN: 0 11 330891 4), produced by the Office of Government Commerce (OGC), does not contain a single overall, detailed process map and it is well worth studying the one shown in Figure 2 as part of your preparation for the examination.

Figure 2 takes each of the major processes and maps the flows of information and products between them.

The acronym in brackets after each product identifies the sub-process that creates it. Remember, for the Foundation Examination, you do not need to go down to the sub-process level in most processes. As part of your preparation, try to produce your own diagram – do not simply rely on the one shown here!

Remember that the main benefit from creating your own summary process diagram will come from the research you will need to do into each process. You will not be allowed to take your summary process diagram into the Foundation Examination, but it will be a useful revision aid and helpful in structuring the content of the Practitioner Examination answers.

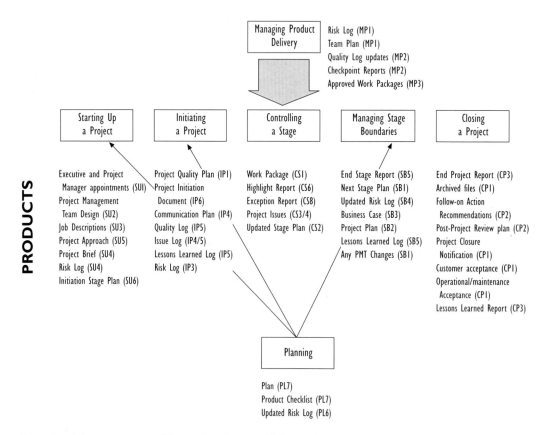

Figure 2 Major processes and flows of products and information

Technique for completing the examination

The paper contains 75 questions, most of which offer four optional answers. Occasionally there will be only two options, e.g. TRUE or FALSE. One (and only one) of the options will be the correct answer. All you have to do is put a tick in the box that corresponds to your chosen answer for that question on the appropriate row on the answer sheet that is provided.

The best technique for the Foundation Examination is to go through the paper in an initial non-stop 'sweep', answering all the straightforward questions to which you know the answers; ignore any long, wordy questions or those that might need some working out. The paper may include 'negative' questions (i.e. '*Which of the following options is FALSE…*') and you might find it easier to return to these at a later time.

When your first sweep is completed you should have most of the questions answered; typically this will take about 15–25 minutes. You can at this stage count up the number of questions you know you have answered correctly to provide a confidence boost – but beware that this might have the opposite effect!

Now return to those more obscure or difficult questions in a second sweep. Many will not be as tricky as they first appeared and, with a bit of common sense and careful reading of the question, you should be able to discount many of the options offered. This may leave you with one option that on re-examination is clearly the correct option. For other questions, you may be left with, say, two options from which you still cannot choose. Leave these and continue the second sweep. You should now feel confident that you are well beyond the pass mark and still have time to spare. Return for a third sweep through those (few) outstanding questions. Review the question and the remaining options. For some, the answer may now suggest itself. For the others, think about them again, but before time runs out, at least make a guess. You should have at least a fifty-fifty chance of being right.

Beware of changing answers you already have – general experience indicates that there are probably as many changes made from correct to incorrect answers as there are from incorrect to correct! If you need to make a change, show it clearly.

You should now be ready to try a Foundation Examination paper – if you have done your preparation work you should be feeling quite confident and ready to tackle the example examination that starts on the next page. Always plan your approach to the real examination – time the completion of the example paper that follows for no more than two days before the examination – you will then be finely honed – with just enough time to review the elements you missed out on but not too much time to cause you to lose the cutting edge you'll need for the real thing.

Good luck!

Sample Foundation Examination Paper

Multiple Choice

Instructions

1   All 75 questions should be attempted.

2   There are no trick questions.

3   All answers are to be marked on the original examination paper.

4   Please use a pen to mark your answers with either a ✓ or ✗.

5   You have 1 hour for this paper.

6   You must get 38 or more correct to pass.

Candidate Number: ....

1. In PRINCE2 what product is used to define the information that justifies the setting up, continuation or termination of the project?

   a) Project Initiation Document ☐

   b) Business Case ☐

   c) End Stage Approval ☐

   d) Project Brief ☐

2. Which product keeps track of Requests for Change?

   a) Request Log ☐

   b) Daily Log ☐

   c) Quality Log ☐

   d) Issue Log ☐

3. What provision in Planning can be made for implementing Requests for Change?

   a) Project and stage tolerances ☐

   b) Contingency plans ☐

   c) A Change Budget ☐

   d) Adding a contingency margin to estimates ☐

4. Fill in the missing phrase from 'a project is a management environment that is created for the purpose of delivering one or more business products according to …'

   a) the Customer's Needs ☐

   b) an Agreed Contract ☐

   c) the Project Plan ☐

   d) a specified Business Case ☐

5. In what sequence would (a) the Project Initiation Document, (b) the Project Mandate and (c) the Project Brief appear in a PRINCE2 project?

   a) a, b, c ☐

   b) b, c, a ☐

   c) c, a, b ☐

   d) c, b, a ☐

6.   Which would require the production of an Exception Report?

   a)   When a Project Issue is received   ☐

   b)   When a Project Board member raises a complaint   ☐

   c)   When a Request for Change or Off-Specification has been received   ☐

   d)   When the current forecasts for the end of the stage deviate beyond
         the delegated tolerance bounds   ☐

7.   Which statement is NOT a fundamental principle of Closing a Project?

   'A clear end to a project ...'

   a)   provides a useful opportunity to take stock of achievements   ☐

   b)   provides an opportunity to ensure that all unachieved goals and
         objectives are identified   ☐

   c)   provides the opportunity to evaluate achievement of all the expected
         benefits   ☐

   d)   is always more successful than the natural tendency to drift into
         operational management   ☐

8.   What is the more common term used in PRINCE2 for 'deliverable'?

   a)   Item   ☐

   b)   Package   ☐

   c)   Product   ☐

   d)   Component   ☐

9.   Which of these items does NOT involve the Project Board?

   a)   Exception Assessment   ☐

   b)   Highlight Reports   ☐

   c)   Project Closure   ☐

   d)   Work Package Authorisation   ☐

10. What name is given to the permissible deviation from a plan allowed without immediate reporting to the Project Board?

    a) Allowance ☐

    b) Contingency ☐

    c) Concession ☐

    d) Tolerance ☐

11. What other control is closely linked with configuration management?

    a) Risk Management ☐

    b) Project Closure ☐

    c) Change Control ☐

    d) Project Initiation ☐

12. Which of these processes does NOT trigger the Planning (PL) process?

    a) Starting Up a Project (SU) ☐

    b) Initiating a Project (IP) ☐

    c) Managing Stage Boundaries (SB) ☐

    d) Controlling a Stage (CS) ☐

13. In a Product Breakdown Structure what category of product is a Highlight Report?

    a) Quality ☐

    b) Specialist ☐

    c) Technical ☐

    d) Management ☐

14. If, after a Quality Review Follow-up Action, an error is still not resolved, what action should be taken?

    a) An Exception Report is made ☐

    b) A Project Issue is raised ☐

    c) An Exception Memo is raised ☐

    d) The review is reconvened ☐

15.   Which of the following is NOT a PRINCE2 definition of a project?

    a)   Has an organisation structure   ☐

    b)   Produces defined and measurable business products   ☐

    c)   Uses a defined amount of resources   ☐

    d)   Uses a defined set of techniques   ☐

16.   What environment does PRINCE2 assume?

    a)   A fixed-price contract   ☐

    b)   A Customer/Supplier environment   ☐

    c)   A specialist environment   ☐

    d)   A third-party environment   ☐

17.   Which feature of PRINCE2 tells the Project Manager where a product is, what its status is and who is working on it?

    a)   Work Package   ☐

    b)   Product Description   ☐

    c)   Checkpoint Report   ☐

    d)   Configuration Management   ☐

18.   In Closing a Project (CP) the project files are archived. What is the explanation given for this?

    a)   To provide useful lessons to future projects   ☐

    b)   Never throw anything away   ☐

    c)   This material may be needed by Programme Management   ☐

    d)   To permit any future audit of the project's actions   ☐

19.   Which of the following statements is FALSE? Project Managers using PRINCE2 are encouraged to …

    a)   establish terms of reference as a prerequisite to the start of the project   ☐

    b)   use a defined structure for delegation, authority and communication   ☐

    c)   divide the project into manageable Stages for more accurate planning   ☐

    d)   provide brief reports to Management at regular meetings   ☐

20.   Which of these is NOT a valid Risk Management action?

    a)   Prevention   ☐

    b)   Denial   ☐

    c)   Reduction   ☐

    d)   Transference   ☐

21.   Which one of these is NOT a PRINCE2 Component?

    a)   Plans   ☐

    b)   Controls   ☐

    c)   Work Package   ☐

    d)   Configuration Management   ☐

22.   Which document lists the major products of a plan with their key delivery dates?

    a)   Product Outline   ☐

    b)   Product Description   ☐

    c)   Product Breakdown Structure   ☐

    d)   Checkpoint Report   ☐

    e)   Product Checklist   ☐

23.   The configuration of the final deliverable of the project is ...

    a)   the sum total of its products   ☐

    b)   the interim products   ☐

    c)   its product description   ☐

    d)   the single end-product   ☐

24.   Which part of a product lifespan is not part of a project life cycle in the eyes of PRINCE2?

    a)   The change-over to operational use of the product   ☐

    b)   Assessment of the value of the product after a period of use   ☐

    c)   The specification of the product   ☐

    d)   Finalisation of the Business Case   ☐

25. What is the first job carried out on receipt of a new Project Issue?

   a) Allocation of priority ☐

   b) Logging ☐

   c) Decision on what type of issue ☐

   d) Impact Analysis ☐

26. Which of these statements is FALSE?

   a) The Project Plan is an overview of the total project ☐

   b) For each Stage identified in the Project Plan, a Stage Plan is required ☐

   c) An Exception Plan needs the approval of the Project Board ☐

   d) At least one Team Plan is needed for every Team Manager ☐

27. Which of the following statements is FALSE?

   a) Customer quality expectations should be discovered in the process 'Starting Up a Project' ☐

   b) A company's Quality Management System becomes part of PRINCE2 ☐

   c) PRINCE2 may form part of a company's Quality Management System ☐

   d) The Stage Plan describes in detail how part of the Project Plan will be carried out ☐

28. Which one of these statements describes the true purpose of Acceptance Criteria?

   a) A justification for undertaking the project based on estimated costs and anticipated benefits ☐

   b) A measurable definition of what must be done for the final product to be acceptable to the Customer ☐

   c) To provide a full and firm foundation for the initiation of a project ☐

   d) To trigger 'Starting Up a Project' ☐

29. How often does PRINCE2 recommend that open Project Issues should be reviewed?

   a) Weekly ☐

   b) At Exception Assessments ☐

   c) At Checkpoint Meetings ☐

   d) On a regular basis ☐

30. What other product is reviewed and updated at the end of each stage apart from the Business Case and Project Plan?

   a)   The Project Mandate   ☐

   b)   The Quality Log   ☐

   c)   The Risk Log   ☐

   d)   The Project Brief   ☐

31. Why is a copy of the Project Issue always returned to the author?

   a)   The author owns it   ☐

   b)   To acknowledge its receipt and entry into the system   ☐

   c)   To elicit further information   ☐

   d)   To notify rejection of the Issue   ☐

32. Which product reviews the benefits achieved by the project?

   a)   Post-Project Review   ☐

   b)   Post-Project Review Plan   ☐

   c)   End Project Report   ☐

   d)   Follow-on Action Recommendations   ☐

33. Which of these statements is FALSE?

   a)   A PRINCE2 project has a finite lifespan   ☐

   b)   A PRINCE2 project has a defined amount of resources   ☐

   c)   A PRINCE2 project may have only activities, i.e. no products   ☐

   d)   A PRINCE2 project has an organisation structure with defined responsibilities, to manage the project   ☐

34. The person best situated to keep an eye on a risk is called its …?

   a)   Supporter   ☐

   b)   Monitor   ☐

   c)   Owner   ☐

   d)   Librarian   ☐

35. Which document reviews actual achievements against the Project Initiation Document?

   a)   End Project Report ☐

   b)   Post-Project Review ☐

   c)   Lessons Learned Report ☐

   d)   Follow-On Action Recommendations ☐

36. In PRINCE2 all potential changes are dealt with as …?

   a)   Configuration items ☐

   b)   Requests for Change ☐

   c)   Project Issues ☐

   d)   Exception Reports ☐

   e)   Action items ☐

37. Which one of these is NOT a key criterion for producing a Product Flow Diagram?

   a)   Are the products clearly and unambiguously defined? ☐

   b)   On what other products is each product dependent? ☐

   c)   Is any product dependent on a product outside the scope of this plan? ☐

   d)   Which products can be developed in parallel? ☐

38. For a Quality Review (QR), when are suitable reviewers identified?

   a)   When the product is passed to configuration management ☐

   b)   In the Project Quality Plan ☐

   c)   During the QR preparation step ☐

   d)   In planning the relevant stage ☐

39. The existence of what product is checked in 'Starting Up a Project' and its initial version finalised in 'Initiating a Project'?

   a)   The Project Mandate ☐

   b)   The Project Plan ☐

   c)   The Project Brief ☐

   d)   The Business Case ☐

40. Which does PRINCE2 regard as the third project interest, given user and supplier as the other two?

   a)   Technical ☐

   b)   Management ☐

   c)   Business ☐

   d)   Quality ☐

41. PRINCE2 lists a number of reasons why it is seldom desirable or possible to plan an entire project in detail at the start. Which of these is NOT one of these reasons?

   a)   A changing or uncertain environment ☐

   b)   A PRINCE2 requirement ☐

   c)   Difficulty in predicting business conditions in the future ☐

   d)   Difficulty in predicting resource availability well into the future ☐

42. In which process is the Project Brief produced?

   a)   Starting Up a Project ☐

   b)   Initiating a Project ☐

   c)   Authorising Initiation ☐

   d)   Authorising a Project ☐

43. When should a Product Description be baselined?

   a)   As soon as it is available in draft form ☐

   b)   When the associated product has passed its quality check ☐

   c)   When the plan containing its creation is baselined ☐

   d)   As soon as it is written ☐

44. A typical Exception Plan covers what period?

   a)   From the problem to the end of the project ☐

   b)   From the problem to the end of the stage ☐

   c)   The work needed to put the project back within its tolerances ☐

   d)   The time needed to produce an Exception Report ☐

45. Stage boundaries may be chosen according to a number of parameters. Which one of the following is NOT one of the parameters?

    a)   The availability of specific resources   ☐

    b)   The sequence and delivery of the products   ☐

    c)   The grouping of products into self-consistent sets   ☐

    d)   The natural decision points for feedback and review   ☐

46. The initial Project Plan is based on the Project Brief, the Project Quality Plan and which other product?

    a)   The Project Approach   ☐

    b)   The Project Initiation Document   ☐

    c)   The project start-up notification   ☐

    d)   The Project Mandate   ☐

47. Which document is a record of some current or forecast failure to meet a requirement?

    a)   Exception Report   ☐

    b)   Off-Specification   ☐

    c)   Follow-On Action Recommendations   ☐

    d)   Highlight Report   ☐

48. If there is a request to change an approved product, and the change can be done within the stage's tolerances, who can make the decision to implement the change?

    a)   Project Manager   ☐

    b)   Team Manager   ☐

    c)   Team member   ☐

    d)   Project Board   ☐

49. 'Controlling a Stage' drives which other process on a frequent, iterative basis?

    a)   Managing Stage Boundaries   ☐

    b)   Approving a Stage or Exception Plan   ☐

    c)   Managing Product Delivery   ☐

    d)   Planning   ☐

50. The Project Quality Plan is written in which process?

    a)   Initiating a Project ☐

    b)   Starting Up a Project ☐

    c)   Managing Stage Boundaries ☐

    d)   Directing a Project ☐

51. What are defined as 'partitions of the project with decision points'?

    a)   Work Packages ☐

    b)   Product Descriptions ☐

    c)   Quality Reviews ☐

    d)   Stages ☐

52. In which lower-level process of 'Controlling a Stage' is the Risk Log updated?

    a)   Reporting Highlights ☐

    b)   Assessing Progress ☐

    c)   Capturing Project Issues ☐

    d)   Examining Project Issues ☐

53. If a question arises on why a particular product was changed, which element of PRINCE2 would be of most help in finding the information?

    a)   Issue Log ☐

    b)   Quality Log ☐

    c)   Configuration Management ☐

    d)   Change Control ☐

54. In which sub-process is a Stage Plan updated with actuals?

    a)   Assessing Progress ☐

    b)   Reviewing Stage Status ☐

    c)   Planning a Stage ☐

    d)   Reporting Highlights ☐

55. In which sub-process are Checkpoint Reports created?

    a)   Executing a Work Package   ☐

    b)   Assessing Progress   ☐

    c)   Reporting Highlights   ☐

    d)   Reviewing Stage Status   ☐

56. Are the following statements true or false?

    – Delegated Project Assurance roles report directly to corporate or programme management

    – In PRINCE2 the Project Manager role must be full time

    – A project management structure is a temporary structure

    a)   All three are false   ☐

    b)   Only the third is true   ☐

    c)   Only the first is false   ☐

    d)   The second and third are false   ☐

57. The process, 'Directing a Project' begins when?

    a)   At the beginning of 'Starting Up a Project'   ☐

    b)   After the start-up of the project   ☐

    c)   At the end of the Initiation Stage   ☐

    d)   Before start-up of the project   ☐

58. Apart from 'Initiating a Project', in which process is the Business Case updated?

    a)   Managing Product Delivery   ☐

    b)   Controlling a Stage   ☐

    c)   Managing Stage Boundaries   ☐

    d)   Authorising a Stage   ☐

59. What does PRINCE2 regard as a prerequisite to the start-up of a project?

    a)   A Project Plan   ☐

    b)   A Project Mandate   ☐

    c)   An appointed organisation   ☐

    d)   Project Initiation Document   ☐

60. In the PRINCE2 document management structure, how many major types of file are recommended?

   a)   One for each Stage   ☐

   b)   Two, Management and Specialist   ☐

   c)   Just the Quality File   ☐

   d)   One per Project Issue   ☐

61. In a Quality Review which role does PRINCE2 suggest must ensure that all reviewers are provided with the relevant review products?

   a)   Producer   ☐

   b)   Scribe   ☐

   c)   Review Chairperson   ☐

   d)   Configuration Librarian   ☐

62. Which of these is mandatory in a PRINCE2 project?

   a)   The use of Team Managers   ☐

   b)   The use of Exception Plans   ☐

   c)   The use of Stages   ☐

   d)   The use of Quality Reviews   ☐

63. The Project Board has three responsibilities towards the management of risk. Which of the following options is the FALSE one?

   a)   Notifying the Project Manager of any external risk exposure to the project   ☐

   b)   Making decisions on recommended reactions to risk   ☐

   c)   Identifying, recording and regularly reviewing risks   ☐

   d)   Striking a balance between levels of risk and potential benefits   ☐

64. What function creates, maintains and monitors the use of a quality system?

   a)   Project Support   ☐

   b)   Quality Planning   ☐

   c)   Quality Control   ☐

   d)   Quality Assurance   ☐

65. Which is not a purpose of configuration management?

 a) To identify products ☐

 b) To create products ☐

 c) To track products ☐

 d) To protect products ☐

66. Which step is NOT part of 'Accepting a Work Package'?

 a) Understand the reporting requirements ☐

 b) Agree tolerance margins for the Work Package ☐

 c) Monitor and control the risks associated with the Work Package ☐

 d) Produce a team plan which shows that the Work Package can be completed within the constraints ☐

67. Which process provides the information needed for the Project Board to assess the continuing viability of the project?

 a) Starting Up a Project ☐

 b) Closing a Project ☐

 c) Planning ☐

 d) Managing Stage Boundaries ☐

68. In which process are choices made about planning tools and estimating methods?

 a) Starting Up a Project ☐

 b) Initiating a Project ☐

 c) Managing Stage Boundaries ☐

 d) Planning ☐

69. In which process are decisions made on Exception Reports?

 a) Managing Stage Boundaries ☐

 b) Closing a Project ☐

 c) Directing a Project ☐

 d) Managing Product Delivery ☐

70. In which process are checks made for changes to the project management team?

   a)   Starting Up a Project ☐

   b)   Managing Stage Boundaries ☐

   c)   Closing a Project ☐

   d)   Directing a Project ☐

71. From the products listed, which one is produced during 'Starting Up a Project'?

   a)   The Project Initiation Document ☐

   b)   The Project Plan ☐

   c)   The Project Quality Plan ☐

   d)   The Project Approach ☐

72. Quality responsibilities, both within and external to the project, are defined in which process?

   a)   Initiating a Project ☐

   b)   Starting Up a Project ☐

   c)   Managing Stage Boundaries ☐

   d)   Directing a Project ☐

73. Approval for the completed products is obtained as part of which process?

   a)   Closing a Project ☐

   b)   Managing Product Delivery ☐

   c)   Managing Stage Boundaries ☐

   d)   Controlling a Stage ☐

74. An Exception Report is produced in which sub-process?

   a)   Taking Corrective Action ☐

   b)   Reviewing Stage Status ☐

   c)   Escalating Project Issues ☐

   d)   Reporting Highlights ☐

75.   Which is the missing section of the suggested Project File, if the others are Organisation, Plans, Business Case and Control?

    a)   Correspondence   ☐

    b)   Daily Log   ☐

    c)   Risk Log   ☐

    d)   Issue Log   ☐

Total Score: ☐

Marking your paper

Now you have completed the sample Foundation Examination paper, check your answers against those shown in Table 1 and look up the page number references in the manual for any questions you answered incorrectly. You should, ideally, be looking for a score of between 60–65 correct answers and completion within 40–50 minutes. Remember, for the actual examination you need to score 38 correct answers in 60 minutes.

Table 1 Answer sheet

Q	Answer	Page	Q	Answer	Page	Q	Answer	Page
1	B	6	26	D	213/214	51	D	234
2	D	312	27	B	254	52	D	106
3	C	168/9	28	B	309	53	C	270
4	D	7	29	D	105	54	A	101
5	B	37/38	30	C	141	55	A	128
6	D	229	31	B	297	56	B	39
7	C	149	32	A	233	57	B	67
8	C	311	33	C	7	58	C	193
9	D	98	34	C	241	59	B	26
10	D	222	35	A	159	60	B	393
11	C	275	36	C	295	61	A	301
12	D	165	37	A	288	62	C	234
13	D	281	38	D	259	63	C	241
14	B	306	39	D	37	64	D	254
15	D	7	40	C	198	65	B	263
16	B	195	41	B	213	66	C	126
17	D	263/4	42	A	37	67	D	134
18	D	154	43	C	284	68	D	167
19	D	3	44	B	215	69	C	85
20	B	244	45	A	237	70	B	136
21	C	187	46	A	51	71	D	27/39
22	E	184	47	B	295	72	A	49
23	A	263	48	D	295	73	B	124
24	B	8	49	C	94	74	C	117
25	B	272	50	A	49	75	C	393

The Practitioner Examination

You must have passed the PRINCE2 Foundation Examination in order to sit the Practitioner Examination.

The Practitioner Examination is a three-hour, open-book examination. Under current rules, you may take the PRINCE2 manual and any notes (including this book) into the examination. A computer or any other electronic reference material is not allowed at present.

On 4 October 2002 a new style of Practitioner Examination paper was introduced as part of continuous efforts to improve the effectiveness of the examination. The following paragraphs explain the new format, indicating the different types of question now being asked, and some suggestions on how to structure answers most appropriately.

The objective of the exam remains the same – to enable a candidate to demonstrate to the examiner an understanding of PRINCE2 and an ability to apply the methodology in an appropriate way in a given set of circumstances described in a scenario.

Structure of the paper

The examination paper will consist of a scenario – no more than one page of A4. There may also be one or two attachments, each one augmenting the scenario information, and being associated with a particular question.

The combination of the scenario, each question and any attachment will always 'position' both the candidate (to consider a particular PRINCE2 role) and the project (in terms of the timescale, e.g. at the beginning, in the middle or at the end of a project). The role to be considered will be at a level suitable for a project manager or one who is aiming to become a project manager.

There are three questions, each worth 50 marks. This gives a total of 150 marks. The pass mark is 75. Some or all of the three questions may be divided into parts. Where this is the case, the portion of the 50 marks allocated to each part will be shown. All questions and part questions should be answered.

PRINCE2 topics commonly addressed

The guidance in the OGC publication, *Managing Successful Projects with PRINCE2*, which addresses the processes, components and techniques of PRINCE2, forms the basis for all the examination questions. Within that broad framework, topics typically examined are:

- The Business Case
- Controls – often focused on specific roles or timeframe within a project
- Monitoring and control of project work by either the Project Board or the Project Manager
- Organisation – structures and roles

- Plans – structures, types and levels, the creation of a Product Breakdown Structure and Product Flow Diagram

- Risk – analysis of a risk

- Quality – throughout the project life cycle or focused on a specific period of the scenario

- Configuration management

- Work Packages

- Tolerance/exception procedure

- Project Issues

- Project Closure

Types of question

Questions are categorised as analytical, contextual or theoretical. Occasionally a question may be a combination of two of these categories.

Analytical questions

Questions in this category may require any of the following:

- specific PRINCE2 products to be created

- comments or recommendations to be made about a PRINCE2 product that is provided as an attachment

- information from the scenario and an attachment to be used in answering the question.

Contextual questions

Questions in this category enable candidates to demonstrate an understanding of how various PRINCE2 topics are linked and might be applied in the circumstances described in the scenario. An example here might be to ask where the Risk Log is updated.

Theoretical questions

Questions in this category provide a means of enabling candidates to demonstrate an understanding of the theory and philosophy of various PRINCE2 topics.

Great care is taken to try to balance the examination papers in terms of level of difficulty and type of question.

Wording of questions

Typically, the questions will ask the candidates to 'identify', 'explain', 'describe', 'comment on', 'list', 'draw', 'create', 'summarise', 'write', 'draft' or 'write notes on' (a particular PRINCE2 document). An alternative style of question is 'How would you/PRINCE2...?' The question may require the candidate to base the answer on one or more aspects of PRINCE2, e.g. processes, components, techniques or management products. The section below addresses how the answers to questions should be tackled.

Questions will make it clear whether they are asking candidates to identify processes (SU, IP) or sub-processes (SU1, IP3). Candidates may choose to use the identifier, write out the sub-process name in full or give a full description of it.

Answering the questions

The first ten minutes (reading time) of the examination is intended to allow the candidate to absorb all the information provided. The invigilator is only allowed to explain a word or phrase whose meaning is difficult for a delegate taking the examination in a language other than their first language. The invigilator is not allowed to relate a question to the PRINCE2 aspects involved. After this period, there are three hours in which to answer the questions. Years of experience tell us it is necessary to remind candidates – **read the question, answer the question**. It does sometimes appear that the candidate has not done one or the other – or neither!!

The candidate's answer, when passed to the examiner, is the only means by which a judgement can be reached on whether the candidate knows and understands the aspects of PRINCE2 being examined. Examiners have no access to the candidate name, training company, or even whether a training course has been attended – candidates are simply identified by a number.

Clear, legible handwriting is a blessing to the examiner! Every effort is made to read what the candidate has written, but if it cannot be read, it cannot be marked.

Structuring the answer

Answers to requests for explanations or summaries can be given in essay form or in bullet points with one or two short sentences of explanation. But if something that you are thinking of writing does not make a PRINCE2 point, do not write it. Remember that it is a PRINCE2 examination, not a general project management one.

Where lists are requested, lists should be created. If the number of items in that list is specified in the question, then only provide that number, not more. For example, if a question asks for six sub-processes that affect the Business Case, the first six listed by the candidate will be taken as the answer. Any extra ones will be ignored. If a question asks for **all** sub-processes, for example, where the Issue Log is studied, do not 'brain-dump' every sub-process of every process. If such a list contains many sub-processes that have nothing to do with the question asked, the marks available are halved.

When asked to draw a diagram, do just that. Do not explain when, by whom and why unless the question asks for this. An example here would be a request to draw product-based planning diagrams.

If asked to create a specific PRINCE2 document, look at the Composition section of the Product Description of that product. This will give you the sub-headings for the document. Do not write **about** the product, about who produces it, in what sub-process or why. Just create the document. If a different part of the question asks the other questions, then fine, give the other information then.

General advice

Fifty marks are available for each of the three questions, giving a total of 150. The requirement for passing the Practitioner Examination is that you must score at least 50% of the marks available, so 75 marks must be gained to achieve a pass. The marks are accumulated for all the questions so it is possible (but difficult) to compensate for one poorly answered question by a brilliant answer to another. Do not be tempted to spend 90–120 minutes on one question about which you feel comfortable. Questions are designed to be answerable in 50–60 minutes. Spending more than this brings in the law of diminishing returns, and you are likely to be spending 10–15 minutes describing in wonderful detail some point that is only worth 1 mark.

Do not use the term, 'etc' in any answer. If there is more to say in answer to the question asked, write it down.

Do not repeat yourself.

Do not refer the examiner to a page in the manual.

Points made in one part of a question may earn marks for another part of the same question if it is clear that you understand the point required (e.g. a point made in answer to question 1B may reveal that the candidate knew a point for which marks were available in question 1A). Marks cannot cross question boundaries (e.g. from question 2 to question 1), because different questions address different aspects of the methodology. If a similar point needs making in another question, make it again.

Start each answer to a sub-question on a new page. This allows you to go back later and add to the answer to a previous question if you have time. You may wish to number your pages as, for example, Q1A–1, Q1A–2, starting from page 1 for each new sub-question. This makes it easier to add extra pages to a question's answer if you go back later.

Answer what to you are the easiest questions or sub-questions first to boost your feeling of confidence, but try not to go beyond the time allowance.

Analytical questions

These require the candidate to demonstrate the ability to apply a particular aspect of PRINCE2 to a set of circumstances described in the scenario, attachments or in the question.

Analytical questions may invite comment on a particular PRINCE2 product. Such products may be:

- an extract from a draft PID
- a Project Quality Plan
- a Quality Log
- a Product Flow Diagram (when compared to a provided Product Breakdown Structure).

This type of question may also require the candidate to create a PRINCE2 product, such as:

- Business Case
- Configuration item record
- Exception Report
- Highlight Report
- Product Description
- Project Approach
- Project Brief
- Project Issue
- Work Package

Contextual questions

Contextual questions test the understanding of the links between sub-processes and between components and sub-processes. A contextual question might require a candidate to list the sub-processes in which a particular PRINCE2 product might be used, e.g. in which sub-processes is the Business Case reviewed?

Theoretical questions

These are straightforward questions on information held either in the manual or course notes. They will test the understanding of the PRINCE2 philosophy and principles. An example of a theoretical question might be to explain the benefits of using the levels of plan proposed by PRINCE2 or why the Business Case is considered as the driving force of a PRINCE2 project.

The problems

Since the introduction of the original PRINCE2 Professional Examinations in January 1997, most of the failures (about 35%) have stemmed from the Practitioner Examination. The reasons are varied, with some candidates simply running out of time and failing to score sufficient marks for the final question. Many failed because they either failed to answer the question posed (and produced an answer that was easier to write but irrelevant!) or were unable to make the all-important connections between the scenario, the question, their experience and the PRINCE2 method.

Sometimes there is little doubt that candidates who fail actually understand the method. Many who fail are sensible middle-managers with at least some practical experience of project management. So the conclusion is that the problems lie with:

- time management
- information retrieval
- examination technique.

Reading time

Under current APM Group rules, candidates for the Practitioner Examination are allowed 10 minutes reading time. During this period you are not allowed to look up or write anything. You will be allowed to highlight and to make notes on the examination question paper. You will not be allowed to refer to the PRINCE2 reference manual, make notes on anything other than the question paper, leave the room or discuss the paper with the invigilator or other candidates.

Use the reading time carefully. Highlight the relevant points the scenario is making. You should aim to fully understand the background and the questions by the time the examination starts.

When reading the questions, underline the verbs to ensure you understand what the question is asking you to do. For example you might be asked to **create** a particular plan or diagram; or the question might ask you to **explain** or **describe** a particular element of PRINCE2. Remember, many candidates who fail the Practitioner Examination do so because they have not answered the question posed.

Time management

Do not waste valuable time repeating the question.

Beside each sub-question is the number of marks available for it. Take a rough allocation of 50 minutes for each question, and then break that down into the time that it is worth spending on each sub-question. For example, if a sub-question is worth only 5 marks, it is worth one-tenth of the 50 minutes (5 minutes) of your time to answer it. So each mark is worth 1 minute of your time.

To ensure that the best use is made of the time available, a reasonable approach is to aim for 'a mark per minute' allowing about 50 minutes to be allocated to each question. This should enable you sufficient time to score around 30–40 marks per question, which is about as many as you can reasonably expect under examination conditions. The questions will indicate a breakdown of the marks available for each part, so allocation of writing time to each part of the question, based on 'a mark per minute', will not be difficult.

But you must be disciplined!

Always leave time to read through your work. This will often reveal missing references and possibly missing key points. Allow about 15 minutes for this – if you find any major omissions and do not have time to write up the full text, just bullet-point the key features and you will be given marks for including them.

Sample Practitioner Examination Paper 1

The examination paper consists of a scenario describing a project, possible attachments (no more than two) and three questions similar to the following.

Scenario

A large sweet-manufacturing company, Candy plc, has been at a disadvantage compared to its competitors due to its outdated technology and lack of control over its own marketing, and this is reflected in increasing costs and declining sales. Candy plc has decided to launch a new packaged chocolate-covered toffee bar to tackle the competition in the 'small bar' market. This will be handled as a PRINCE2 project and you are the Project Manager.

The Project Board consists of the Marketing Director (Senior User), Head of Production (Senior Supplier) and the Financial Director (Executive). An overall investment of £3.5m has been allocated for this venture, agreed by the Financial Director.

In the past Candy plc has sold direct to supermarket chains and wholesalers. The wholesalers sold the products on to small retailers. The supermarkets expected a lower price that gave them a 15% profit margin. Wholesaler and small retailers both expected a profit margin of 10%. This left Candy with a 15% profit margin. Marketing suggests that going direct to the small retailers and offering a 12% profit margin would provide Candy with a 25% profit margin. Sales to supermarkets would continue unchanged. For this product Candy plc will perform its own marketing and a new sales process is being developed within the project. The design and creation of the marketing material are needed for a comprehensive launch of the product. A decision is also needed on the target audience for the marketing material before it can be designed and distributed.

Candy plc needs to successfully launch the chocolate bar via direct sales while maintaining its current level of quality and customer satisfaction. The launch date is 2 January (8 months after the project start date). Breakeven point must be within 24 months of the launch. Marketing believe that direct sales will increase Candy plc's market share by 10%.

A feasibility study established that Candy could produce the new bar and its wrapping with current equipment, but recommended investment in new equipment at a cost of £250,000 that will allow production of the expected volumes for year 2 onwards. Using current equipment would require a night shift to produce the required volume at an additional cost of £185,000 per year.

To launch the product the project will generate an advertising campaign that will include both television and press advertisements. These will need to conform to corporate standards and include the corporate logo.

The new production equipment needs to be ordered, delivered and installed. Agreements with suppliers need to be made for the provision of materials. These include the wrappers, boxed containers and the ingredients. The wrappers and boxes will need to comply with the size limits of the equipment. A trial of the production line will be needed, and sufficient supplies will need to be distributed to the sales outlets before the launch.

Question 1

(a)   Select a risk associated with the scenario and using the PRINCE2 approach carry out the risk analysis steps, giving reasons for each step of the analysis for the risk. **(26 marks)**

(b)   Make proposals for the management of the risk. **(8 marks)**

(c)   Identify the processes in which PRINCE2 states specifically that the Project Manager will examine risks and explain why the examination is done. **(16 marks)**

Question 2

Based upon your submission to the Project Board at the end of the start-up process, the initiation stage has been authorised. You are now in a position to plan the project. **Using only the products identified in the scenario**, draw a Product Breakdown Structure for the project **showing Specialist products only** and create a Product Flow Diagram from the Product Breakdown Structure. **(50 marks)**

Question 3

The project has moved on four months and is now in its final stage. See the attached memo from the Marketing Director. The attached Highlight Report, issued three weeks ago, is also for your information.

(a)   Draft the initial Issue Log entry for the production of miniatures. **(7 marks)**

(b)   Carry out an impact analysis based on the information available to you. **(22 marks)**

(c)   Assuming that after the impact analysis this change is confirmed as high priority, list the PRINCE2 processes you would use and what would be done in each to support this request. **(21 marks)**

Highlight Report

CANDY BAR PROJECT   7 October

To: Distribution List as per Communications Plan

Period Covered: 7 September to 7 October

Budget status

	Planned expenditure to date	Forecast total expenditure	Tolerance available
Project (£) 3.8m	3.4m	3.84m	0.1m
Stage (£) 0.6m	0.2m	0.64m	0.1m

Schedule status

	Planned end	Current forecast	Tolerance available
Project	7 January	7 January	Zero
Stage	7 January	7 January	Zero

Products completed during period

Marketing material

Installed equipment

Actual or potential problems and risk update

None

Products to be completed during the next period

Completed production trial

Distributed launch material

Launched Candy bar

Project issue status

None outstanding

Budget & schedule impact of any changes

Has already cost of £40,000 in overtime payments

MEMO

From: The Marketing Director

To: The Project Manager

Date: October 28th

This morning I briefed my staff on the new Candy bar and how we will launch the product. During the briefing we received the results of some research that reveals that if we were to issue one box of miniature versions of the product as samples to go to all the shops in advance of the full marketing launch campaign, this would increase our customer base by 12%. The miniatures would be needed two weeks prior to the launch date. I have already had a word with the Production Director who pointed out that production of the miniatures would have to be done after the trial run. In elapsed time his senior engineer believes that it would need 4 weeks to modify the production line and 3 weeks to produce the miniatures. Marketing costs would rise by £75,000. Production costs would be £150,000. As there is no plan to produce the miniatures, I am raising this with you as a change that is urgently required. Could you please prepare the necessary paperwork for consideration?

An examiner has marked the sample answer below. The ticks and comments in italics are from the examiner to show where the answer was good and where it could have been better.

Question 1

(a)　Select a risk associated with the scenario and using the PRINCE2 approach carry out the risk analysis steps, giving reasons for each step of the analysis for the risk. **(26 marks)**

(b)　Make proposals for the management of the risk. **(8 marks)**

(c)　Identify the processes in which PRINCE2 states specifically that the Project Manager will examine risks and explain why the examination is done. **(16 marks)**

Candidate's answer

Q1(a)　The PRINCE2 risk analysis steps are:

- identify

- evaluate

- generate possible risk actions

- select an appropriate risk action.

OK, but not actually asked in the question.

Risk identification: The late addition of the requirement to have miniature versions of the bar ready in advance of the marketing launch campaign brings a risk that the miniatures cannot be produced in time and will delay the launch. ✓ ① *(No category mentioned.)*

Evaluation: This risk is evaluated as a high probability with high impact. Reasons: The Production Director has already forecast a seven-week activity to produce the miniatures and there is zero time tolerance available. ✓ *(Half marks awarded for the reasons for the assessment as no explanation given for the impact if this risk occurred.)*

Possible risk actions: (a) The whole campaign could be slipped by the time required for the miniature production. (b) The campaign could go ahead without the miniatures, i.e. drop the Request for Change. (c) Full candy bars could be substituted for the miniatures. These would be available and save the cost and time of changing the production equipment. There would be a cost of the bars, but this should be less than the one-off costs of the miniatures. ✓ ③ *(To get the 4 marks for discussion of effect the marking scheme awards marks for statements on what **each** action would achieve. This is because this information plus cost-effectiveness of risk would be used to inform the next step in the risk analysis: risk selection. In this answer the effect of each action has not been discussed, i.e how actions will deal with the risk in terms of reducing, preventing, transferring the risk or providing contingency. However, one mark was awarded for recognition in (c) that cost of risk actions could be less than the risk occurring.)*

Selected risk action: I would recommend option A. The current launch date has already missed the Christmas sales period and January is probably a low-sales time, with everyone having stocked up on chocolate for Christmas. It might be better to aim for the Easter sales peak, allowing more time tolerance to overcome any new equipment, supplies or marketing campaign problems. ✓ ④ *(There is no one correct answer here – the candidate has made a sensible suggestion and supported it with sound reasoning.)*

The candidate scored 16 out of a possible 26 marks.

Q1(b) The risk management activities are:

- plan

- resource

- monitor

- report.

I would revise the Project and Stage Plans to meet a later launch date. The plans would include the extra activities and resources (engineering plus materials) for production to create the miniatures, and I would allow time beyond the seven weeks currently forecast because this job has not been done before and the equipment is new. I would look for extra Checkpoint Reports from production during the miniature creation to spot any problems as early as possible and I would also ask the Senior Supplier's assurance role to make regular checks. I would ensure that the work was broken down into a number of smaller 'products' or points in the equipment modification – again as early checkpoints. I would have checks entered in my Daily Log, not only to check on progress, but also to emphasise to the production staff that there was management focus on this work. I would expect the Project Board to ask for more frequent Highlight Reports during this period and maintain regular liaison with marketing. If major problems appeared that might impact the new target date I would recommend that we switch to option C. ✓ ⑥ *(Full marks awarded for planning, resourcing, monitoring and reporting.) The candidate scored 8 out of 8.*

Q1(c)

- SU – identify risks in the Project Brief ✓ ⑧ *(This is sufficient to gain marks for SU4.)*

- IP3 – revise risks in the light of the Project Plan ✓ ⑧

- SB4 – revise risks in the light of the completed current stage and the next Stage Plan ✓

- CP2 – add any on-going risks to the Follow-on Action Recommendations ✓

The candidate scored 7 out of 16 marks.

Question 2

Based upon your submission to the Project Board at the end of the start-up process, the initiation stage has been authorised. You are now in a position to plan the project. **Using only the products identified in the scenario**, draw a Product Breakdown Structure for the project **showing Specialist products only** and create a Product Flow Diagram from the Product Breakdown Structure. **(50 marks)**

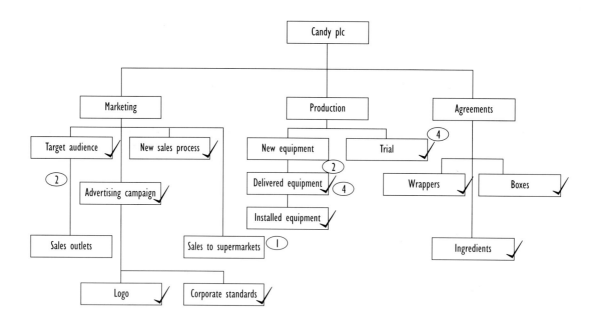

(11 out of a possible 18 scenario products identified)

Figure 3 Product Breakdown Structure

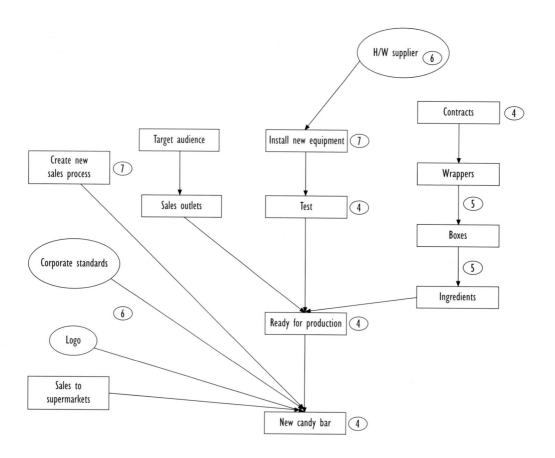

Figure 4 Product Flow Diagram

Question 2

Examiner's comments

(The point numbers 1, 2, 4, 5, 6 and 7 refer to the numbers circled in the given diagram.)

1.   The marking scheme awards marks for products identified in the scenario. While products identified by a candidate could be relevant to the scenario, project marks are not awarded for these as this would unduly favour candidates familiar with such projects. In other words we are looking for the candidate to demonstrate his or her expertise by **applying the technique to the scenario text***. Application of the technique to a similar real-life example will not gain the candidate any marks and more than likely will result in loss of marks.*

Of the 18 possible products the candidate has correctly identified 11. Marks were not awarded for the product Sales to Supermarkets. Sales to Supermarkets will occur after launch and is outside the scope of this project.

2.   There are one-to-one links in the PBS - one mark was lost for this. Also the breakdowns of New Equipment and Delivered Equipment are not genuine 'this consists of'. They are 'this is followed by', so this loses another mark.

3.   (General observation.) While some products are missing, the major areas have been covered – full marks.

4.   There are inconsistencies between the PBS and PFD. One mark lost for the top product of the PBS and end product of the PFD not being the same. Two further marks lost for three products in the PFD but not in the PBS (Test, Ready for Production and Contracts) and two products in the PBS not in the PFD (Delivered Equipment and Trial).

5.   There are a number of dependency errors because of incorrect dependencies between supplier agreements for ingredients, boxes and wrappers. No dependencies between the latter are described in the scenario.

6.   Three marks awarded for the use of an ellipse for externals and Corporate Logo and Standards were identified as externals. One mark was deducted because H/W Supplier is a resource not an external product.

7.   One mark lost for the inclusion of two activities instead of products in the PFD.

8.   (General observation.) Eleven products gains 11/18 × 15 = 9 marks.

The candidate scored a total of 30 out of 50 marks.

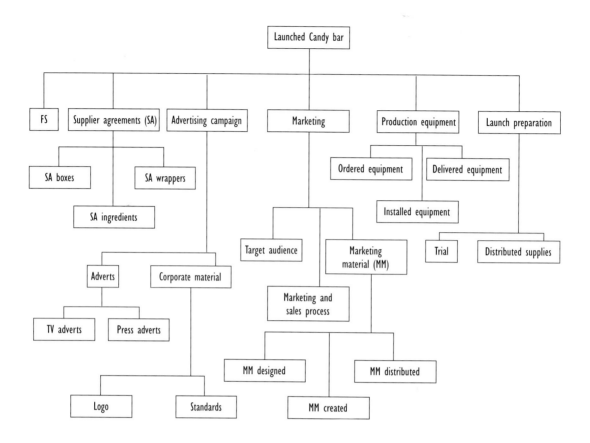

Figure 5 Sample answer: Product Breakdown Structure for the Launched Candy Bar Project

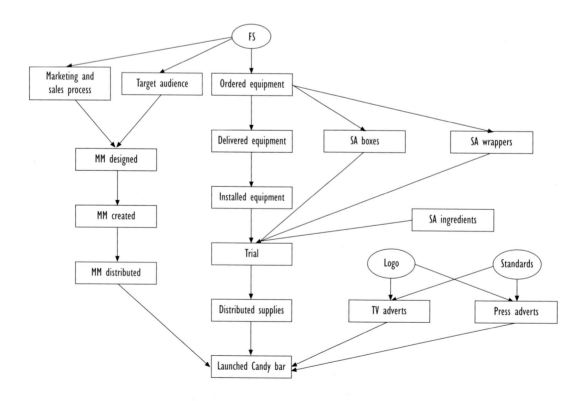

Figure 6 Sample answer: Product Flow Diagram for the Launched Candy Bar Project

Question 3

The project has moved on four months and is now in its final stage. See the attached memo from the Marketing Director. The attached Highlight Report, issued three weeks ago, is also for your information.

(a)   Draft the initial Issue Log entry for the production of miniatures. **(7 marks)**

(b)   Carry out an impact analysis based on the information available to you. **(22 marks)**

(c)   Assuming that after the impact analysis this change is confirmed as high priority, list the PRINCE2 processes you would use and what would be done in each to support this request. **(21 marks)**

Candidate's answer: Question 3(a)

Issue Log entry

Project Issue Number CANPI23 ✓

Type: RFC ✓

Author: Marketing Director ✓

Date Identified (today) ✓

Date of Last Update (today) ✓

Description ✓

There is a need to produce sample boxes of miniatures of the new chocolate bars in advance of the marketing launch campaign. Sufficient would be needed to supply one box to all shops to be targeted in the campaign.

Status: Open ✓

Examiner's comments

The sample answer followed the headings in the Issue Log Product Description and gave a sensible entry for each. The candidate scored 7 out of 7.

Candidate's answer: Question 3(b)

Impact analysis

The priority of the request is 1 – a 'must'. This is clear from the memo from the Marketing Director. *(Quite correct, but not what is asked by the question. The priority is initially entered by the author, so it would already be there. Reassessing priority is not done until the impact analysis has been completed, and so is not part of the analysis.)* The Production Director says that the work would add 4✓ weeks to the Stage Plan. *(Factually wrong. The available information – see memo from Marketing Director – says that it would take 4 weeks to modify the production line and 3 weeks to produce the miniatures.)* Tolerances✓ ⑤ will be exceeded. The extra cost of £225k will exceed project cost tolerance so that will certainly include exceeding stage cost tolerances. The extra time required will cause time tolerances to be exceeded at both stage and

49

project level. *(This is a good statement about tolerances.)* There are costs✓ ⑥ associated with the change, so the Business Case✓ would change. *(Too brief an answer. Information is available in the material to be more specific. There was no attempt to answer the question, 'What would have to change?', nor was any impact on risks assessed.)*

The candidate only scored 7 out of 22 marks.

Candidate's answer: Question 3(c)

The Project Issue impact analysis is done in CS4. *(Again, correct, but not what the question is asking. The answer should start after the results of the impact analysis have been reviewed and a request made to implement the change.)* The results are reviewed in CS5✓ ⑧. The Project Manager may decide that the change can be handled within tolerances (CS7). *(True, and there is a case for the examiner to decide whether to award a mark in the 'extras' row, but in reality the Project Manager should realise that there is no way he/she can manage their way out of such a large deviation. This answer is really trotted out from the manual rather than any real consideration of whether it might apply in this case.)* If not, he will escalate it to the Project Board✓ in an Exception Report✓ ⑧ (CS8) ✓ ⑧ *(Any answer to a question that includes the Exception Report should show understanding of what it is, i.e. its composition.)* The Project Board will ask for an Exception Plan✓ *(No mention of DP4)* in an Exception Assessment. *(The answer did not cover the actions if, as is the case here, it is project tolerances that are forecast to be exceeded. There was also no mention of the additional actions if a new plan is created – updating the BC and risks.)*

Only 4 out of 21 marks scored.

Sample Practitioner Examination Paper 2

The original answers were all produced under examination conditions. The answer paper has been reviewed by the APMG's Chief Examiner and comments added.

Scenario

An American yachting enthusiast has just bought a successful British boatyard on the south coast. The firm has a long order book for the luxury catamarans that it builds. Six vessels are in build, contracts signed, and stage money received. The previous owner has arranged to sell the site currently used by the boatyard. The new owner has leased a hangar on a former airfield, six miles inland, and all the workforce (a foreman, five shipbuilders and four office staff) are willing to move to the new site. The foreman has inspected the hangar and believes that it is perfectly adequate for the work.

You are a professional, independent Project Manager. You have been asked by the new owner to manage the whole project to set up the new premises and move the company to the new site.

The boatyard machinery has to be dismantled, moved and reassembled at the new site by the boatyard shipbuilders. A more powerful electricity supply needs to be installed by the local electricity company to supply electricity to the new site to cope with the demands of the machinery.

At present access to the new site is restricted to light traffic because of major roadworks. The local council expects to finish the work by 10 December, and the new road will make it easy to move heavy loads to and from the site.

An office is to be constructed inside the hangar. The shipbuilders have offered to build this. The foreman has estimated that it would need five shipbuilders to build the office after he has designed it. Sub-contractors would then install cabling to provide electricity from the new supply to the office and then decorate the office before the office move could take place.

You are tasked to prepare plans for the move to commence on 1 December and be completed by 11 January. The move has to be completed in six weeks because the new owners of the boatyard site intend to start building work on a marina then. They are adamant that there will be no site access for your client after the six weeks.

Your project is responsible for transportation of the six catamarans to the new site. A firm has been approached to carry out the move of the vessels, and has estimated that each yacht move would require two days. The contract firm has only one crane and one yacht transporter suitable for the work. Your project must get a contract signed with the local firm for this work.

Questions

Q1(a) Demonstrate your understanding of the scope of the project by drawing a Product Breakdown Structure for the specialist products for the Project Plan.
(18 marks)

Q1(b) Create a Product Flow Diagram from the Product Breakdown Structure.
(18 marks)

Note: The examiner will award up to 14 extra marks for these diagrams where candidates show a good understanding of the product-planning technique by showing realistic products, based on the scenario, in their diagrams. No extra writing or additional diagrams are required.

Q2(a) Select three risks associated with the scenario and using the PRINCE2 approach carry out a risk analysis giving reasons for each step for each risk.
(23 marks)

Q2(b) Make proposals for the management of each risk. **(10 marks)**

Q2(c) Identify the major events at which the Project Manager will examine risks.
(17 marks)

Q3(a) Draw an organisation structure for the project, naming the people who would fill each role. **(22 marks)**

Q3(b) Explain briefly any other project organisation options that you might consider. **(14 marks)**

Q3(c) Suggest suitable stages for the project and give reasons for your choice.
(14 marks)

Answer script

Question 1(a)

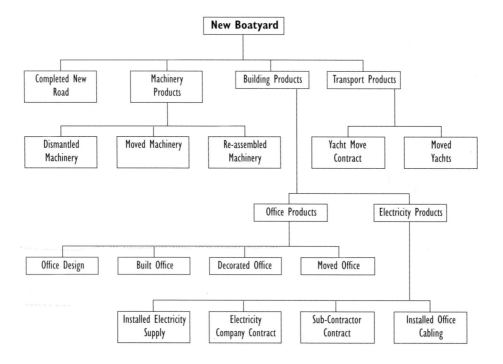

Figure 7 Product Breakdown Structure

Marker's comments

This is excellent. Good breakdown, sensible products. Captured all the products mentioned in the scenario. All the breakdowns are clearly 'this consists of', with no examples of falling into the trap of breakdowns that mean 'this is followed by'. The only question is whether or not the scenario stated that contracts would be needed for the improved power supply and the later sub-contractor. Full marks.

Question 1(b)

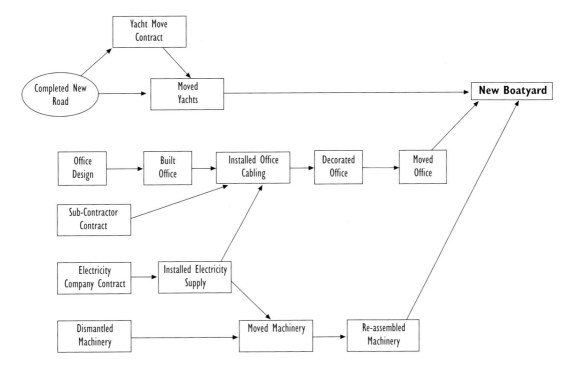

Figure 8 Product Flow Diagram

Marker's comments

A good PFD with only a couple of errors. The completed new road is also a dependency of 'moved machinery', and the yacht move contract is not dependent on the completed new road. Otherwise good. The external is correctly identified. The 'installed electricity supply' could have been another external if it had to be done anyway, rather than as a result of a contract within the project's bounds. The arrows are clear, almost made unnecessary by the good left–right flow. Good point was the use of 'new boatyard' as the top of the PBS and the final product in the PFD. The answer gets full marks for accurate match between PBS and PFD names and no use of activities. Only lowest-level products in the PBS have been transferred to the PFD, making it very easy to ensure that all correct products move between the two diagrams. The external product was also correctly listed in the Product Breakdown Structure as well as shown in the PFD.

Question 2(a)

Risk can be defined as uncertainty of outcome. All projects face risks and the project must determine the level of risk it is prepared to tolerate.

This project has many risks inherent due to the short timescale and dependencies on external factors. They fall into the risks categories of strategic/commercial and technical/operational/infrastructure in the main.

Marker's comments

The two paragraphs above say sensible things, but nothing that would gain them marks in the examination. They are too general. Remember, the question simply says 'select three risks'.

Three risks in this project are:

1   delay to commencement of transportation of machinery and vessels due to roadworks not finishing until 10 December

2   delay to vessels transportation due to the contract firm having only one crane and yacht-transporter – legal/regulatory (contracted arrangements)

3   vessels in build not being completed on time due to boatyard move, e.g. machinery does not work when assembled – technical/operational/infrastructure (increased dismantling time).

Marker's comments

Three clear risks. You could say that the first risk is of the roadworks not finishing until 10 December, which would have the effect of delaying commencement of machinery and vessel transportation; similarly with the other two risks, but the markers would accept these.

The risk log shown is based on the product description outline in PRINCE2. The scores are 1 = low, 2 = medium, and 3 = high. The tolerance score is the probability and impact multiplied together to evaluate the level of risk. Any risk scoring 6 or above would be above the risk tolerance line and not acceptable. These require risk actions to be identified and costed. Any contingency actions should have a contingency budget allocated for use should they occur.

Marker's comments

The table [see Table 2] is a useful shorthand way of expressing a lot of information – and reminding the candidate of required entries. Very often candidates give all details for the first risk, but forget one or two entries by the time they are doing the third risk. The table would have been lacking without the following explanation of what the possible range of scoring was and what the tolerance score meant. Remember the manual only uses the high, medium and low categories, so use of anything else should be explained.

Reasons

Risk 1

Road projects are frequently delayed, but tighter contracts are reducing this and so the probability is 2. The impact is 2 because there are 4 weeks between completion of the road and project completion – only 12 days are needed to move the yachts.

The Executive is the owner as this is a risk from outside the project.

Table 2

RISK	Transportation delay due to roadwork completion delay	Transportation delay due to firm having only one crane and one transporter	Vessels in build not completed on time due to project problems. Risk to business, e.g. machinery does not work when reassembled
Category	Strategic/commercial	Strategic/commercial	Technical/operational/ infrastructure
Impact	2	3	3
Probability	2	2	1
Score	4	6	3
Proximity	Close	Medium	Later
Response 1	Maintain close links with council regarding finish dates	Plan for minimum of 3 vessels moved by Xmas to give float time	Identify plans to recover from any delays after move or be ahead prior to move
Response Type	Reduction	Reduction	Contingency
Response 2	Negotiate extended site access from new owners if risk occurs	Plan for transportation during weekends and bank holidays if needed due to delays	Identify priority order for building yachts
Response Type	Reduction	Contingency	Reduction
Response 3	Plan transportation to commence after road due to be completed	Contract penalties for delay	Discuss any acceptable delays with purchasers and keep them informed of plans
Response Type	Contingency	Transference	Acceptance
Response 4		Identify alternative if needed	
Response Type		Prevention	
Owner	Executive (new owner)	Project Manager	Foreman

Risk 2

The probability of the crane or transporters breaking down and delaying the project is medium as the firm is undertaking this work regularly and relies on its machinery for its business viability. The impact would be high as there will be no site access after the 6 weeks.

The Project Manager is the owner, as he/she is best placed to monitor the risk.

Risk 3

The probability of this happening is low as the move has been planned and it is likely to have been discussed with purchasers. If it happened it would have a high impact as there are considerable costs incurred to the business due to loss of reputation and loss of income. This is why the Senior User has been identified as the owner. I have suggested this would be the foreman as he would have the specialist knowledge to represent all the aspects of the project and would also be impacted by the outcome.

Marker's comments

Three very clear reasons for the estimation of the risks. A common fault made by many candidates is to forget to give reasons, just the table of values. Again the table layout avoided another common fault: failure to mention that PRINCE2 requires each risk to have an owner. The examiner will always expect a sensible suggestion as to who the owner should be – derived from the scenario. The only thing missing from the answer is risk evaluation: the balance of the cost of the risk occurring against the cost of the possible risk actions.

Question 2(b)

Risks need to be managed and the first step in this is to identify them and log them.

The three risks identified then need planning, resourcing, monitoring, reporting and budgeting.

The risks would be logged as soon as identified, not as part of risk management.

Risk 1

Responses for countermeasures would be:

1 maintain close links with council

2 negotiate extended site access

3 plan transportation later than road completion.

Resourcing will need time of the Executive for 1, Project management for 2 and 3, so costed for by time.

Risk 2

Responses would be:

1 plan minimum three vessels moved by Xmas

2 contingency to use weekends and bank holidays if delays incurred

3 contract penalties for delays

4 identify alternative method, e.g. airlift between sites.

Resourcing will need time of Project Manager for 1, 2, 3 and 4 and costs of this time. Additional contingency costs are needed for 4.

Risk 3

Responses would be:

1 plan to catch up from any delays and/or be ahead prior to moves

2 identify buildings order by date urgency/priority

3 discuss acceptability of delays with purchasers and keep informed of plans.

Resourcing will require time of foreman for 1 and 2, with 3 being carried out by either the Executive or someone delegated by them. Again costs associated with this time need to be planned.

Marker's comments

A choice of risk responses is part of risk analysis, not risk management. Marks can, at the examiner's discretion, be awarded for comments made in a different section of the same question. In this case, these comments would be added to those in the marking scheme in the answer to Q1(a). Marks cannot, however, cross question boundaries, e.g. a point made in answer to Q2 cannot earn marks in Q1. The resourcing comments made at the end of each set of actions show who would be needed to take action, plus the costs. The comments seem intended to cover the first two steps of risk management – planning and resourcing.

All three risks need to be monitored and reported on. I recommend that a risk profile is used and shown in Highlight Reports to Project Board. Checkpoint Reports from the teams will be frequent and have risk status identified. The Project Manager will review risks frequently with some daily when the proximity is close.

As a minimum they are updated at each stage end but this is a high-risk project and the Project Manager will monitor them more frequently.

Marker's comments

The answer made two points about reporting (Checkpoint Report and Highlight Report) and two about monitoring (End Stage Assessment and daily reports). The answer will thus get some marks for this part, but it would have been clearer to mention that Highlight Reports are from the Project Manager, the Project Manager using the Daily Log to record moments at which to monitor risks and then record any status change in the Risk Log. The Project Manager reports on risk status in the End Stage Report, which will allow the Project Board to monitor risks as part of their End Stage Assessment.

Question 2(c)

The Project Manager needs to keep a close eye on the risks in this project to ensure all vessels and machinery are moved while access is available to the new site.

Marker's comments

This is correct, but a general comment that would not earn marks. Remember, if a sentence doesn't make a specific PRINCE2 point, don't write it.

Risks are at first identified when preparing the Project Brief and the Risk Log is established. The Risk Log will then be updated in IP3 when refining the Business Case and risks. Further risks come to light and more information is available for risks already identified as more detail is gathered about the project. The planning process requires risks to be analysed prior to completion of any plan. The Project Quality Plan (PQP) and Project Plan have been developed and so new risks will have been identified.

Marker's comments

The answer is a mixture of process identifiers (IP3) and process descriptions (preparing the Project Brief). Both are acceptable and earn marks.

The Project Manager will continually assess information from checkpoints CS2 and add information to the Risk Log where appropriate. He/she also captures and examines Project Issues, CS3 and 4, which are likely to identify some further risks.

Marker's comments

CS3 does not update the Risk Log, but marks would be earned for CS2 and CS4.

This project is likely to have many Project Issues arise due to reliance on third parties (electricity and transportation) and interdependence on another project (road).

At each point that stage status is reviewed (CS5) the Risk Log is reviewed to ensure that it is up to date and there are no risks to completion of the current stage. When preparing for ESAs the risks are updated by the Project Manager in SB4 to go to the Project Board.

Time is critical in this project and tight tolerance is likely to be in place. This is appropriate as there are high risks associated with time. The Project Manager will examine the risk – particularly those associated with time – prior to every Highlight Report to the Project Board (CS6). Any changes in status or new ones will be in the report.

Marker's comments

There were marks available for identifying that time was critical and that there should be a tight time tolerance connected to keeping a close eye on the risk associated with any time slippage.

Question 3(a)

Table 3 Organisation Structure

EXECUTIVE	New Owner
SENIOR USER	Foreman, shipbuilder
SENIOR SUPPLIER	Yacht transportation company, electricity company
PROJECT ASSURANCE	Project Board
PROJECT SUPPORT	Office staff
TEAM MANAGERS	Foreman, shipbuilder, external suppliers

Reasons

User – The foreman will be impacted by the outcome as will the shipbuilder. There are two Senior Users because there is a need to balance the Project Board and there are two suppliers.

Senior Supplier – There are two major suppliers to the project and these are represented on the Project Board.

Executive – The new owner has the business interests and the accountability for the project.

Project Assurance – No one in the scenario has suitable skills to fulfil this role. It is a small project with teamwork essential. I recommend that the Project Board members undertake their own project assurances. Responsibility always rests with the Project Board.

Project Support – will be carried out by the office staff, in terms of filing and organising for configuration management. It is unlikely that they will have the skills needed to do more.

Team Managers – There are several Team Managers needed for this project. Some are external and some internal. Each major piece of work will have a Team Manager identified, as there are discrete work packages in this project. The foreman is in a position to act as Team Manager for the office design but I recommend the shipbuilder as Team Manager to build it.

Marker's comments

The organisation structure is acceptable and the above reasons were good. Note, however, that the question did not ask for reasons. Therefore just the organisation structure would have been enough to gain the marks. Only give reasons if the question asks for them. Otherwise you are wasting precious time writing words that will not earn extra marks.

Question 3(b)

Other options are to have a single Senior Supplier and Senior User (foreman and contract yacht transportation company) as they are the main risk areas in the project. A supplier group could be formed to have input from the external suppliers.

Marker's comments

From the suggestion of foreman and contract yacht transportation company, the candidate does not mean to combine the roles, just balance the 'opposing' numbers on the Project Board. The sample answer has a suggestion that the new owner take on the Senior User role as well as Executive role. As Project Board members are supposed to be able to commit resources, the new owner may feel that only he can do this, not the foreman. When you consider who the suppliers are, it seems unlikely that they could be formed into a group. The yacht transporters, local council and electricity company seem to have little in common at a management level. It is difficult to imagine any one of these suppliers controlling the others as sub-contractors.

The Project Manager could do Project Support if the office staff do not have time due to the additional work involved in the move. The Project Manager could also act as Team Manager for the internal work packages. He is likely to be up to date with what is happening in each work package, as it is a small project. I do not recommend he act as Team Manager for external work packages.

It is possible to consider bringing in external Project Assurance, but with a short timeframe project in a small team who work well together, I do not recommend this additional overhead to be necessary. The Project Board are likely to have the skills for both project management standards (Executive) and quality assurance (Senior User and Senior Supplier).

Marker's comments

This seems very unlikely, and no reasons are given to suggest what skills the external Project Assurance would need to have. Would it be assurance for the Executive, i.e. someone watching the pennies, someone with logistics skills? If such a suggestion is to be made, there would have to be much more detail in terms of what assurance was to be sought.

Question 3(c)

Stages for this project need to coincide with natural decision points. Each time the Project Board meets they are tackling decisions and giving direction to the project to keep it in control.

Marker's comments

Again a general comment, not earning marks.

All projects need an initiation stage (PRINCE2 recommends it).

Marker's comments

The remark about initiation earns marks.

Stages

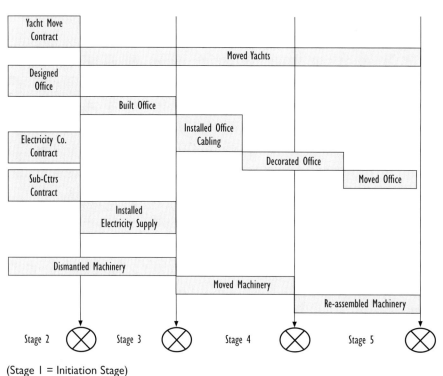

Figure 9

Stage 1 – Initiation – firm foundation.

Stage 2 – Once contracts are ready, ask the Project Board (PB) to sign them off and agree the office design.

Stage 3 – Once the electricity is installed and machinery is dismantled, is the PB satisfied that the new site is ready for the machinery to be moved? Has the new road been completed in time?

Stage 4 – Once the machinery is moved, is the PB satisfied it is ready for reassembly? I recommend this coincides with the first three yachts being moved prior to Xmas.

Stage 5 – Is the PB satisfied that all the yachts have been successfully moved and the new boatyard premises fit to resume boat building?

There are frequent stages to keep under tight control, as this is a high-risk project. The stage boundaries allow PB involvement at potential risk points.

Marker's comments

There were marks available for mentioning that risk and time monitoring were major influences on stage choice, so this last sentence picked those up. Stage 5 looks like project closure – the CP process and DP5. Project closure is not a stage, merely a Project Board control point.

Summary: The paper would have scored very high marks – in excess of 100 out of the 150 available. Only the small issues pointed out in the notes would have resulted in missed marks. Possibly the most important observations are:

●   Answer the question, not less than is requested, but equally not more

●   Do not write general comments. The candidate did well to avoid long essays, which often involve general comments that make it difficult for the examiner to spot items that will earn marks.

And finally ...

If you have managed to get this far you are as ready for the PRINCE2 examinations as you are ever likely to be. It remains only to wish you the little bit of luck that we all need to make a success of any venture in life. If you are still not confident of your knowledge of PRINCE2 or your ability to convince an examiner that you are able to apply it to a given situation, you should consider attending an APM Group accredited training event and, perhaps, try to gain a little more experience in using the method.

Practising writing answers to typical project management situations, using the approaches suggested in this book, will certainly help to prepare you for the examination and help develop your ability to respond to a problem using a structured method.

The sample scenario above can also be used to set yourself other questions – for example '*Describe how you would handle any changes required during the project*' and '*Write a Product Description for one of the products in your Product Breakdown Structure*'.

You can also use your own experience to generate a scenario and questions – this is sometimes the easiest way to start your preparation. Try to identify the key topics for each question first; then answer the questions (or at least some parts of them). Remember that you will not score all the marks for just identifying and explaining the PRINCE2 topic, but that you must relate the topic to the scenario.

Good luck with your preparation.

December 2003

Index